Just Mom and Me Having Tea

A Devotional Bible Study for Mothers and Daughters

Mary Murray

HARVEST HOUSE PUBLISHERS
Eugene, Oregon 97402

Scripture quotations are taken from the *International Children's Bible, New Century Version,* copyright © 1983, 1986, 1988 by Word Publishing, Dallas, Texas 75039. Used by permission.

Design and production by Katie Brady

To Sophia with love

Just Mom and Me Having Tea
Copyright © 2001 by Mary Murray
Published by Harvest House Publishers
Eugene, Oregon 97402

Murray, Mary, 1961–
Just mom and me having tea / Mary Murray.
    p. cm.
ISBN 0-7369-0426-3
    1. Daughters—Religious life—Juvenile literature. 2. Mothers and daughters—Religious aspects—Christianity—Juvenile literature. [1. Mothers and daughters—Religious aspects—Christianity. 2. Christian life. 3. Prayer books and devotions.] I. Title.

BV4860 .M87 2001
248.8'45—dc21   00-063468

Printed in the United States of America.

06 07 08 09 / RDC-BG / 10 9 8 7 6 5

❁ Foreword ❁

I can't think of too many things I enjoy more than spending time with my daughter, Abigail. I've only known her for ten years, but in that short time I've learned that I want at least 50 more. We learn more about each other every day, and one of the things that's most clear to me is that if we're going to have years of fun and fellowship ahead of us, we need all the fresh ideas we can get. My goal for us is to continue to cultivate and enjoy this relationship with each other and in the Lord until we're both gray with age. To do that, her memories of the type of mother I was are very important.

Now to my delight, my friend, Mary Murray, has given me an avenue to having even more special time with Abby. Mary's heart for children and her understanding of their needs and wants astound me. Many years past, Mary was my son's kindergarten teacher. Her patience and kindness with him and the creative ways she worked with her class still linger in my mind. Now in this book Mary has given me a tool I can use daily. The Scriptures, prayers, and activities give Abby and me a specific time together, and the fabulous tea party ideas are only the start. Having a journal page where I can write my thoughts is very special. It's a book that Abby can hold onto until she has children of her own, and it will remind her of the time we shared.

Deuteronomy 4:9 says, "Only give heed to yourself and keep your soul diligently, lest you forget the things which your eyes have seen, and lest they depart from your heart all the days of your life; but make them known to your sons and daughters."

What better way to cement God's truth in our daughters' young hearts than to give them opportunity to study the Word with their mothers, and then to see their mothers living out that truth in joy?

I'm so excited and thankful for Mary's hard work on this book. I know God is going to use it in a powerful way in my life and, I trust, in the lives of many mothers and daughters.

Warmly in Christ,

Lori Wick

Lori Wick

✿ Introduction ✿

As a busy mom with two children, I am constantly looking for ways to spend quality time with my son and daughter that will enhance our relationship and enrich their understanding of God and His Word. In an effort to strengthen the bond I have with my daughter, Sophia, I prayerfully developed this Bible study guide to help us grow closer in the Lord together.

We know that the God-given relationship between a mother and daughter is special and unique and is one that requires consistent nurturing, attention, and care. *Just Mom and Me Having Tea* will help you establish a loving relationship with your daughter, enhance your communication, and build trust between the two of you as you get together on a regular basis to share insight, read Scripture, pray, and spend time together in fellowship. There are tea party ideas included in each chapter to add lots of fun to this unique mother/daughter Bible study.

Just Mom and Me Having Tea is designed for moms on-the-go like you and me. All you need is about 30 minutes a day to complete one devotional lesson each week.

We'll cover six topics that are important in the lives of young girls: Friendship, God Made Me Special, My Family, Knowing Our Awesome God, Loving God's Word, and Helping Others. The art projects and craft ideas included in each chapter will help reinforce each topic of study and will make learning fun and meaningful to your daughter. The journal activities will enhance your relationship as both mother and daughter reflect on their lives and share what they're learning. (Moms with younger daughters may want to take dictation and write their daughter's words for them, on the Daughter's Reflection pages.)

Upon completion of this book, be sure to put it in a special place. You will want it for a keepsake and will enjoy looking back on it in the years to come. It will be a great way to rekindle cherished memories and to measure the growth that has taken place in your lives and in your relationship with each other.

Just Mom and Me Having Tea is ideal for a group Bible study as well. Invite some other mother-daughter pairs to meet with you on a weekly basis. Complete a lesson together at home, then gather with the other mothers and daughters and talk about what you've learned as you go through each lesson in a group setting. You will develop new friendships that are grounded in the Word of God, and you will learn a lot from each other as you grow closer to the Lord.

My prayer is that *Just Mom and Me Having Tea* will help you and your daughter begin to develop a lifelong friendship that is rooted and established on the Word of God.

Sincerely,

Mary Murray

Mary Murray

Our Covenant

We promise to be faithful to each other and to God. We promise to work together through this book and talk with and listen to each other. We promise to honor, respect, and pray for each other. We promise to love God above all else.

_____   _____
Mom   Me

_____
Date

Love the Lord your God with all your heart, soul and strength. Always remember these commands I give to you today. Teach them to your children. Talk about them when you sit at home and walk along the road. Talk about them when you lie down and when you get up (Deuteronomy 6:5-7).

✿ Getting Ready for a Tea Party ✿

There are six suggested tea party celebrations in this book, one to correspond with a chapter topic. Each one has a special theme and lots of suggested ideas and activities to make your tea party a memorable experience. You can make your tea party as simple or as elaborate as you like by trying some or all of the ideas on the page. Pick and choose the activities that work best for you and your daughter.

Read through the activity page before each tea party and note what specific materials and supplies you may need. Gather the supplies and materials so you have them at your fingertips when it's time for the tea party.

General Supplies

Here is a list of some basic supplies that you will need for any of the suggested tea parties.

I suggest storing some of the tea party supplies in a box or drawer that is within your daughter's reach so that she can help get out the supplies and set up the tea table.

Supplies

- Teapot
- Teacups and saucers
- Serving tray
- Napkins
- Sugar and lemon
- Spoons
- Small dessert plates
- Assortment of tea bags

Include some of these supplies to make your tea party extra special:

- 🍵 Decorative tablecloth
- 🍵 Cloth napkins
- 🍵 Pretty placemats
- 🍵 Lace gloves
- 🍵 A table centerpiece (a suggested centerpiece idea can be found on each tea party page)
- 🍵 Decorative invitations
- 🍵 Festive napkin rings

Tea Alternatives

You don't have to drink tea at your tea party. Try some of these other favorite beverages:

> Hot cocoa, pink lemonade, fruit juice, lemon water, chocolate milk, flavored ice tea, soda pop, etc.

Young girls may enjoy some of the sweeter flavored teas such as apple cinnamon, orange spice, strawberry, or mixed berry.

Gathering Supplies

You can often find pretty and inexpensive tea party supplies at second hand stores and rummage sales. Make a day of it and have fun shopping together.

Purchase some plain colored teacups and a ceramic teapot. Work together to decorate the cups and teapot with permanent markers or acrylic paints.

❀ Contents ❀

God Made Me Special

> You made me and formed me with Your hands. I praise You because You made me in an amazing and wonderful way. What You have done is wonderful. I know this very well.
> (Psalm 119:73, 139:14)

Seeing myself as being someone special takes clear thinking. I can't be full of pride over who I am, but God's love does set me apart. And I'm learning that if I know I'm special in God's sight, my daughter will follow in my footsteps.

— ❤ Lori Wick

God Made Me!

Write your name here:

Praise and Thanksgiving

Praise God because he is great!... Lord, I will thank you with all my heart (Deuteronomy 32:3b and Psalm 138:1a).

Praise God for creating you. Thank Him for making you just the way you are. Talk to God about the things you like about yourself. Ask Him to help you and your mom grow closer to each other as you work through this book together.

Story Time

It Was Very Good

One Sunday afternoon Sophie invited her best friend, Marissa, over for lunch. "Wow, your mom is the best cook in the world!" Marissa said. "That homemade soup was good. Those muffins were good, and even the salad was good. But Sophie, those chocolate chip cookies were the best! They were very good!"

Marissa really liked the lunch she had at Sophie's. She said everything was "good," but the chocolate chip cookies were even better; they were "very good."

That's a good reminder of what God said when He created everything in our world. God made the sun, moon, stars, land, water, plants, birds, fish, and more. Everything God made was "good." He said so Himself. But after He made people, God said it was "very good." He saved the best for last.

The Bible Says,

God looked at everything he had made, and said it was very good (Genesis 1:31).

God made you, and that makes you a very special girl. Remember that as you work through the activities in this lesson.

Let's Get Started

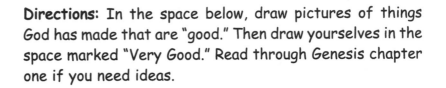

Directions: In the space below, draw pictures of things God has made that are "good." Then draw yourselves in the space marked "Very Good." Read through Genesis chapter one if you need ideas.

Good

Very Good

Sharing Our Thoughts

Most important, love each other. Use all wisdom to teach and strengthen each other (Colossians 3:14, 16b).

Read the questions below. Share your answers with each other and/or write down your answers in the spaces below.

1. What are two or three things you like about yourself?

2. What are you good at doing?

3. How can you show God you are thankful for your body and your talents?

Activity Time

Me Box

Directions:

1. Use the construction paper, scissors, glue, and stickers to decorate the outside of the box and label it with your name.

2. Think about what makes you special and gather an assortment of items from the list below. Place them inside the box.

3. Copy and complete the poetry starter (below) onto a pretty piece of paper and place it in the box with your collection.

4. Share the things in your Me Box with your family this evening.

Materials needed:
- empty box with lid
- construction paper
- markers or crayons
- stickers
- scissors
- glue
- pencil
- items that show and tell about what makes you special (see list below).

Stuff to include in your Me Box:

- pictures of yourself, family, and friends

- your Bible

- any awards or certificates you may have earned

- objects that show what hobbies you enjoy. For example: fabric and thread if you enjoy sewing, a piece of fishing tackle if you enjoy fishing, etc.

- objects that show what you're good at doing. For example: a tennis shoe if you're good at running, a paintbrush if you're good at painting, etc.

God Made Me!

I'm glad God gave me _____.

He made me very special.

He made my _____ .

He gave me beautiful_____.

He created me different than _____.

I'm happy because I can _____ and _____ and _____.

God is great for giving me _____.

I'm really good at _____.

I'm glad that I can _____.

God must love me a lot for making me
_____.

I'm glad God made me just as I am.

Getting Into God's Word

Open my eyes to see the wonderful things in your teachings...How I love your teachings! I think about them all day long (Psalm 119:18, 97).

Every day this week read about how wonderful it is that God made you! Read each Scripture passage and answer the question(s). Share your answers with each other.

Day of the Week	Verse	Something to think about. . .
Monday	Psalm 119:73	*After working hard to make something with your own hands, how do you feel about what you have made? How do you think God feels about making you?*
Tuesday	Genesis 1:26,27	*What makes you more special than the animals, birds, and fish that God created?*
Wednesday	Psalm 100:1-4	*How can you show God you are happy that He made you?*
Thursday	1 Corinthians 3:16	*God's Spirit lives in you and that means your body is pretty special. How can you help take care of your body, God's temple?*
Friday	Ephesians 4:24	*In what ways are you becoming more like God?*
Saturday	Philippians 4:13	*What are some things that are difficult for you? How does it help you to know that you can do anything because of Jesus' strength in you?*
Sunday	Ephesians 1:5	*God chose you because He loves you. What are some things about you that are pleasing to God?*

Talking with God

Then you will call my name. You will come to me and pray to me. And I will listen to you (Jeremiah 29:12).

Pray this prayer or write your own, thanking God for creating you. Then spend some time praying together as you praise God for His wonderful works.

Stuff We Need to Talk to God About

Think of one thing you need prayer for. Write it down in the space below. Talk about it together, and then remember to pray for each other this week.

Dear God,
We love You. Thank You for creating Mom and me. Thank You for making us in your image. Lord, You are great. We're glad You gave us Your Word so that we could learn to be more like You. Thank You for loving us so much. In Jesus' name we pray. Amen.

Daughter   **Mom**

Pray with all kinds of prayers, and ask for everything you need (Ephesians 6:18).

Mother's Insight

Teach older women to be holy in the way they live...In that way they can teach younger women (Titus 2:3,4a).

Share your personal thoughts with your daughter regarding one or more of the following questions or statements. In the space below write down some of your thoughts and ideas.

1. Share with your daughter about the things that make her very special to you.

2. Tell why you're glad God made you just as you are. Include what you like about yourself.

3. If you've ever wanted God to change something about your physical appearance or abilities, how did you learn to love and accept yourself in that area?

4. What Scriptures have helped you realize that God created you perfectly and wonderfully?

❤I'm Very Special!❤

Today I praise God for:

Praise and Thanksgiving

Praise God because he is great!...Lord, I will thank you with all my heart (Deuteronomy 32:3b and Psalm 138:1a).

Thank God for making you different from everyone else. Ask God to teach you how to be thankful for the way He made you. Ask Him to help you work hard at using your talents and gifts to show your love for Him. Talk to God about how you can love people who are different from you.

Story Time

Different and Beautiful

Olivia and her mother were in the garden pulling weeds and watering the plants. They had many flowers in their backyard including geraniums, roses, pansies, daisies, lilies, and black-eyed Susans. Olivia loved to dig in the dirt and help her mom water the flowers. They always wore their matching sun hats and gardening gloves when they worked outside.

"Mom, out of all the flowers we have, I think I like the lilies best. But the daisies are pretty too. So are the roses. I think they're all beautiful, even though they're all different."

"Olivia, I'm glad you said that. Remember the other day when you said you wished you had longer hair like your friend Lisa? And I said, 'You have beautiful hair even though it's not like Lisa's'?"

"Yes, I remember, but I kind of do like her hair better than mine."

"Well, Olivia, just like He made all these flowers different, God made people different too. Each of us may look different, act different, and be good at different things, but we're all beautiful in God's eyes.

"Olivia, I'm glad God made you beautiful and different. I love you just the way you are, and so does God."

The Bible Says,

I praise you because you made me in an amazing and wonderful way. What you have done is wonderful (Psalm 139:14).

Let's Get Started

Directions: In the space below, draw two girls that are different from each other. Then give them each a name and fill in the blanks at the bottom of the page.

This is _____.

She is good at _____.

She likes _____.

Sometimes it's hard for her to _____.

God made her different and beautiful!

This is _____.

She is good at _____.

She likes _____.

Sometimes it's hard for her to _____.

God made her different and beautiful!

Sharing Our Thoughts

Most important, love each other. Use all wisdom to teach and strengthen each other (Colossians 3:14, 16b).

Read the questions below. Share your answers with each other and/or write down your answers in the spaces below.

1. How are you and your mom alike and how are you different?

2. Tell about some of your favorite things, like colors, foods, hobbies, books, songs, etc.

3. What can you do to help each other be thankful for the way God made you?

Activity Time

Different and Beautiful

Materials needed:
- one large sheet of construction paper
- markers or colored chalk
- picture of yourself
- a variety of types and textures of paper
- scissors
- glue
- crayons

Directions:

1. Print *God Made Me Different and Beautiful* at the top of a sheet of construction paper.

2. Use the different types of paper to make pretty flowers in a garden setting.

3. Try cutting, folding, curling, and tearing the paper to make each flower different.

4. Draw stems and grass and other details with the colored chalk or markers.

5. Cut around the edges of the photograph so that only your face shows.

6. Paste it in the center of one of the flowers.

7. Hang up your picture to remind yourself that God made you beautiful and different.

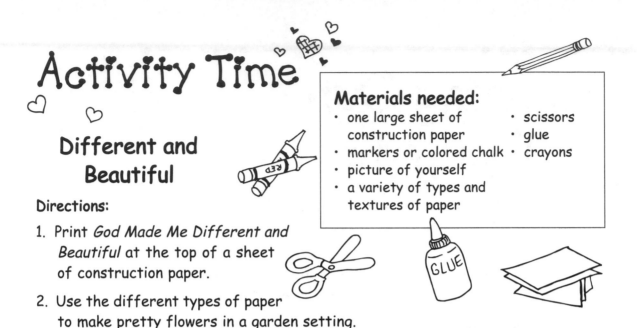

God Made Me Different and Beautiful

❀ Getting Into God's Word ❀

*Open my eyes to see the wonderful things in your teachings.... How I love your teachings!
I think about them all day long (Psalm 119:18,97).*

Read every day this week about how God made you a very special person! Read each Scripture passage and answer the question(s). Share your answers with each other.

Day of the Week	Verse	Something to think about. . .
Monday	Psalm 139:13,14	*What is wonderful about how God made the human body? What is especially wonderful about the way He made you?*
Tuesday	Romans 12:6	*What are some of the gifts God has given you?*
Wednesday	Psalm 139:1-4	*What can you do to make sure your words, actions, and thoughts will please God?*
Thursday	Colossians 3:23	*What should you think about whenever you play a game or use your special gifts and talents?*
Friday	Romans 8:9-11	*How will your life look different from other people's lives if God's Spirit lives in you?*
Saturday	Colossians 3:3,4	*Isn't it great to know that you will be with Jesus some day? What do you think it will be like on that day?*
Sunday	1 Corinthians 2:16	*If you have the mind of Christ, what are some things you should think about?*

Talking with God

Then you will call my name. You will come to me and pray to me. And I will listen to you (Jeremiah 29:12).

Pray this prayer or write your own prayer, thanking God for making you special.

Stuff We Need to Talk to God About

Think of one thing you need prayer for. Write it down in the space below. Talk about it together, and then remember to pray for each other this week.

Dear God,
We praise You for creating us. Thank You that You made each of us different from each other and very special. We know that we are special to You, Father. Help us to be thankful for the way You made us. Thank You that I am good at _____ and Mom is good at _____. I really like how You gave me _____ and You gave Mom _____. You sure did make us wonderful. Amen.

Daughter	Mom

Pray with all kinds of prayers, and ask for everything you need (Ephesians 6:18).

A Daughter's Reflection

God began doing a good work in you. And he will continue it until it is finished when Jesus Christ comes again (Philippians 1:6).

Read these questions aloud. Talk with your mom about your answer to each question. Draw or write about your answers to some of the questions in the space below.

1. What three things do you like best about yourself?

2. What can you do to show God that you are thankful for the way He made you?

3. How do you take care of yourself to show honor to your own body because you belong to God?

Mom and Me
Our First Formal Tea Party

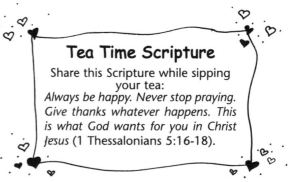

I pray that your life will be strong in love and be built on love (Ephesians 3:17).

Make It Special

In addition to the tea party supplies and suggestions listed on pages 6 and 7, you can add a special touch to your first Mom and Me Tea Party with some of the supplies and ideas listed on this page.

❀ Table decorations: Print **MOM AND ME** around the border of a sheet of construction paper in your best writing. Set it in the center of the table along with a vase of fresh flowers and a framed photo of the two of you. Sprinkle small paper hearts or candies around the centerpiece.

❀ Cover the table with a nice tablecloth.

❀ Light candles and play soft music.

❀ Get out your most formal teacups, saucers, and teapot. If you have cloth napkins, use them for this special occasion.

❀ Put on your best formal gowns, fancy hats, and some extra special jewelry for this grand event. Invite your daughter to wear a formal gown from her "dress up" collection or yours.

❀ Purchase inexpensive pairs of white lace gloves for each of you to wear to the tea party. (You can always wear them again at another tea party.)

Tea Time Scripture
Share this Scripture while sipping your tea:
Always be happy. Never stop praying. Give thanks whatever happens. This is what God wants for you in Christ Jesus (1 Thessalonians 5:16-18).

Try This

Try one or more of these activities to make your tea party extra special and more meaningful.

M&M Game: Put six M&Ms in each tea cup at the beginning of the tea party. Spill out your cup of candy. Look at the pieces of candy. If the "M" is facing up, give a positive comment to the other person. If the "M" is facing down, give yourself a positive comment. Then eat the candies.

Share with your daughter about the day she was born. Tell her how special that day was to you.

Write a love note to the other person on a decorative sheet of stationery. Roll it up and tie it with a pretty ribbon. Display these in the center of the table. At the end of the tea party, read your love notes aloud to each other.

String necklaces of sweet, O-shaped cereal or colorful plastic beads. Wear your necklaces during the tea party.

Talk about a favorite memory of the two of you together.

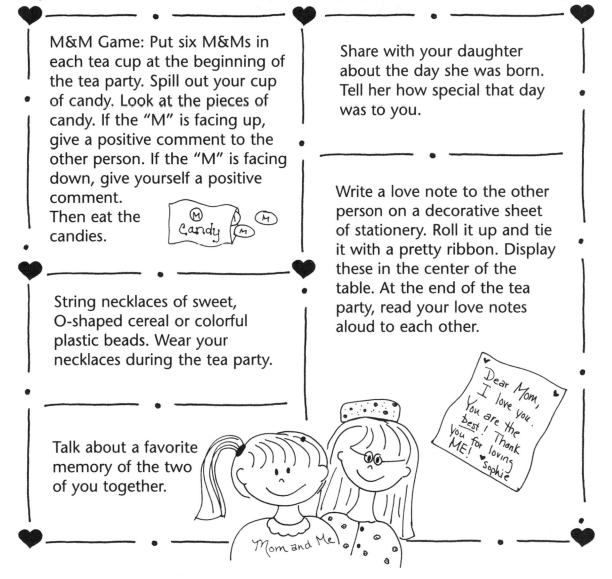

Menu Suggestions

Choose one or more of the following menu items. Work together to prepare the snack and then serve it at the tea party along with the tea, juice, or other favorite beverage.

Heart Biscuits

Open a can of refrigerator biscuits. Form each piece of dough into the shape of a heart. Bake as directed. Serve with butter or jam.

Or use the pieces of dough to spell out **MOM & ME** on a cookie sheet and continue as stated above.

Sweet Treats

Frost vanilla wafers or graham cracker quarters with canned frosting. Top with sprinkles, colored sugar, or the leftover M&Ms.

Mom and Me

Chapter Two

Friendship

> You are God's children whom he loves. So try to be like God. Live a life of love. Love other people just as Christ loved us. Christ gave himself for us (Ephesians 5:1).

Having a daughter as a friend is about as sweet as it can get. If I can do anything in her life so that she will someday be friends with her own daughter, I'll have done a great work.

— ♥ Lori Wick

Friendship Is a Gift from God

Today I praise God for:

Praise and Thanksgiving

Praise God because he is great!...Lord, I will thank you with all my heart (Deuteronomy 32:3b and Psalm 138:1a).

Praise God for His goodness and thank Him for loving you. Thank God for your family and friends. Ask Him to help you be grateful for your friends and to teach you how to be a good friend.

Story Time

In the Same Class

"Mom, guess what?" Shelly shouted as she came running into the kitchen. "Elisa and I have the same teacher next year! We both have Mrs. Taylor." Shelly was very excited. Her mother shared her excitement, "I'm happy for you, Shelly. I bet Elisa is happy too."

Shelly and Elisa are best friends. They like to do everything together. They live two blocks away from each other and spend lots of time riding bikes, roller-skating, and catching frogs in the creek in their neighborhood. They met in preschool when they were both four years old. Now they are going to be in second grade together.

How about you? Do you have a friend that is special to you? God has blessed us with friends at school, church, work, in our neighborhoods, and within our homes. Friendship is a wonderful gift from God. He gave us friends to help, encourage, love, and share with us. He also gave us friends to help us grow closer to Him. God is our best friend. He created us, and He knows us better than anyone else. God loves us all the time, no matter what!

The Bible Says,

Two people are better than one. They get more done by working together. If one person falls, the other can help him up. But it is bad for the person who is alone when he falls. No one is there to help him. If two lie down together, they will be warm. But a person alone will not be warm. An enemy might defeat one person, but two people together can defend themselves. A rope that has three parts wrapped together is hard to break (Ecclesiastes 4:9-12).

Let's Get Started

Directions: Read Ecclesiastes 4:9-12 again. Draw or write about why it is good to have friends.

Draw a picture of one of your friends. Write her name in the space below and explain why you like her.

Daughter

Mother

My friend_____.

My friend_____.

Sharing Our Thoughts

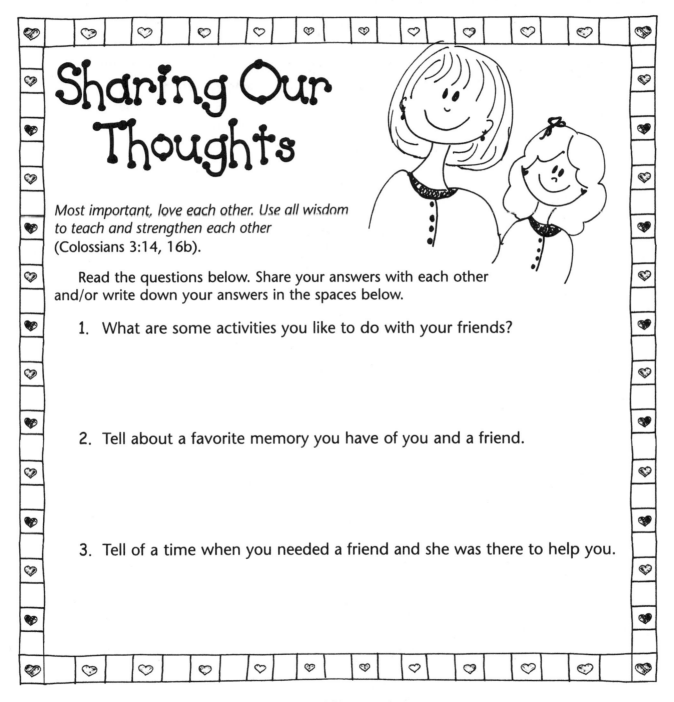

Most important, love each other. Use all wisdom to teach and strengthen each other (Colossians 3:14, 16b).

Read the questions below. Share your answers with each other and/or write down your answers in the spaces below.

1. What are some activities you like to do with your friends?

2. Tell about a favorite memory you have of you and a friend.

3. Tell of a time when you needed a friend and she was there to help you.

Activity Time

Friendship Banner

Materials needed:
- one 12x4-inch piece of colored construction paper
- black marker
- tape
- 26-inch piece of yarn

Directions:

1. Cut the corners off one end of the paper (as shown).

2. Make a half-inch fold at the other end of the paper.

3. Lay the string underneath the fold, then tape the fold shut.

4. Tie the ends of the string together so you can hang the banner on a wall or doorknob.

5. Use the marker to print *Friends* at the top of the banner and *Thank You, God* at the bottom of the banner.

6. Take turns writing the names of your friends all over the banner.

7. Hang the banner in your room as a reminder that friendship is a gift from God.

Getting Into God's Word

Open my eyes to see the wonderful things in your teachings.... How I love your teachings! I think about them all day long (Psalm 119:18,97).

Read about friendship every day this week! Read each Scripture passage and answer the question(s). Share your answers with each other.

Day of the Week	Verse	Something to think about. . .
Monday	Psalm 106:1	How can you show God you are thankful for the good gift of friendship? Name one friend you are especially thankful for. Tell why.
Tuesday	Philippians 4:19	Tell how God has met your needs by giving you a friend at school, church, home, work, or in your neighborhood.
Wednesday	John 15:12	What can you do to show a friend you care?
Thursday	Philippians 1:3,4	What are some things you can pray about for one of your friends?
Friday	1 Peter 3:8,9	How can you get along with your friends better?
Saturday	Romans 12:13	How can you share your things or your home with your friends? Do you know someone who needs a friend? What can you do to help her?
Sunday	Matthew 17:1	Name three of Jesus' best friends. What do you think Jesus liked to do with His friends?

Talking with God

Then you will call my name. You will come to me and pray to me. And I will listen to you (Jeremiah 29:12).

Pray this prayer or write your own prayer thanking God for friends. Then spend some time praying together as you ask God to help you become a good friend.

Stuff We Need to Talk to God About

Think of one thing you need prayer for. Write it down in the space below. Talk about it together, and then remember to pray for each other this week.

Dear God,
Thank You for all the good gifts You've given to us. Thank You most of all for giving us our friends. It's great to have a friend to talk with and to do things with. It's fun to go special places and just be together. Thank You for giving us Jesus. He is the best friend of all. And Lord, thank You that we, as mother and daughter, are also friends. Help us to learn how to love our friends like You love us. Amen.

Daughter	Mom

Pray with all kinds of prayers, and ask for everything you need (Ephesians 6:18).

36

Mother's Insight

Teach older women to be holy in the way they live...In that way they can teach younger women (Titus 2:3,4a).

Share your personal thoughts with your daughter regarding one or more of the following questions or statements. In the space below write down some of your thoughts and ideas.

1. Share with your daughter about a time when you saw her being a good friend to someone else.

2. What have you learned over the years about the value of friendship?

3. Tell of a time when you truly appreciated a friend that God placed in your life.

4. What wisdom can you share about choosing friends?

Friendship God's Way

Today I praise God for:

Praise and Thanksgiving

Praise God because he is great!...Lord, I will thank you with all my heart (Deuteronomy 32:3b and Psalm 138:1a).

Talk to God about how much you love Him. Thank God for giving you each other, and then praise Him for giving you friends. Choose one special friend and thank God for putting her in your life.

Story Time

My Bike Is Better than Yours!

Kali and Mary were very good friends. They played on the same softball team, they both liked doing art projects, and they were in Sunday school class together. They would invite each other over quite often and usually had a great time together. But, sometimes Kali and Mary didn't treat each other very well. Once in a while Kali would say things like, "You're not very smart." Or "That's stupid." Or "My bike is better than yours." And sometimes Mary would say things like, "I don't want to play with you." Or "You're not very nice." Or "I'm better at doing cartwheels than you are." When Kali and Mary talked this way to each other, things didn't usually go very well.

How about you? What kind of friend do you think God wants us to be? The Bible has a lot to say about how to treat other people. There are many people in the Bible that we can learn from. Jesus, Himself, was the perfect example. He loved people with all of His heart, and He taught others how to love like He did. In fact, He commands us to love others. Let's see if we can become more like Jesus as we learn to love our friends His way.

The Bible Says,

A friend loves you all the time (Proverbs 17:17a).

Remember this verse as you learn more about what it means to be a good friend to others.

⋅❀⋅Let's Get Started⋅❀⋅

Directions: Draw or write about some of the things Jesus did that shows He was a good friend to others.

Jesus was a good friend to others because...

Sharing Our Thoughts

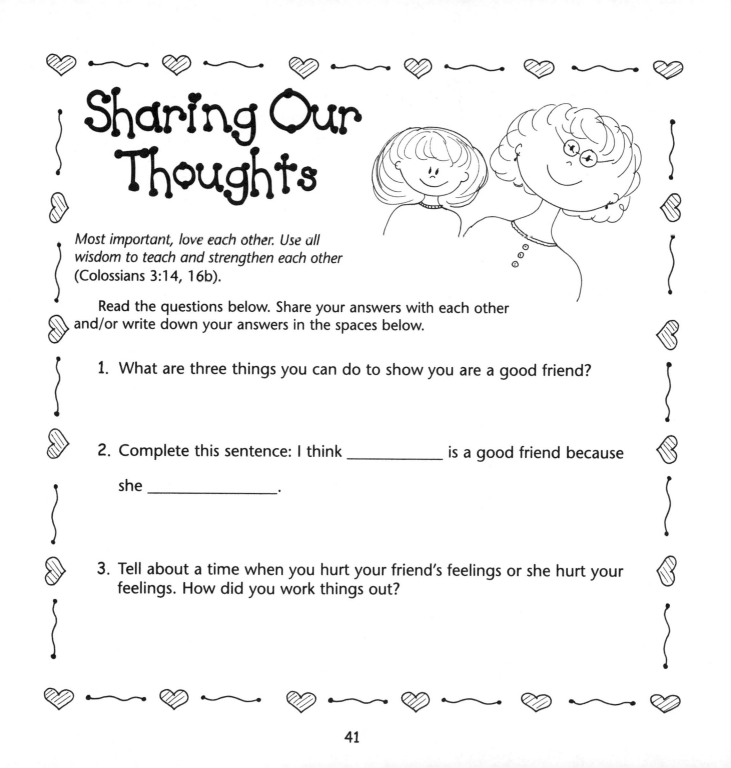

Most important, love each other. Use all wisdom to teach and strengthen each other (Colossians 3:14, 16b).

Read the questions below. Share your answers with each other and/or write down your answers in the spaces below.

1. What are three things you can do to show you are a good friend?

2. Complete this sentence: I think _____ is a good friend because

   she _____.

3. Tell about a time when you hurt your friend's feelings or she hurt your feelings. How did you work things out?

Activity Time

Materials needed:
- paper plate (for cardboard circle)
- black marker   • scissors
- 4-inch piece of colored cardboard
  (cut from a cereal box)
- paper fastener

Time to Be a Friend

Directions:

1. Print *A friend loves you
   all the time (Proverbs 17:17a)* in the center
   of the paper plate.

2. Print the numbers 1 through 12 around
   the border of the plate to make the face
   of a clock.

3. Talk about different things friends do for each other.

4. Read the sentence below out loud and fill in the blank as you print a word
   beneath each number.

It's time to _____. Suggested words:
forgive, love, listen, share, help, pray,
encourage, be kind, thank God, cry, play.

5. Cut two clock hands from the colored
   cardboard.

6. Print *MOM* on the minute hand. Print
   ME on the hour hand.

7. Attach the hands to the center of the
   plate with the paper fastener.

8. Take turns moving the hands around
   the clock and giving examples of times
   when a friend needs to love, listen,
   forgive, encourage, etc.

Getting Into God's Word

Open my eyes to see the wonderful things in your teachings...How I love your teachings! I think about them all day long (Psalm 119:18,97).

Read every day this week about how to be a good friend! Read each Scripture passage and answer the question(s). Share your answers with each other.

Day of the Week	Verse	Something to think about. . .
Monday	Romans 12:15	When a friend is happy or sad, what can you do to show that you care about her? Tell about a time when you shared in a friend's happiness or sadness.
Tuesday	1 Corinthians 13:4	What are two things you can do to show love to a friend? Give an example of each.
Wednesday	Ephesians 4:29	What are some things you can say to a friend that will make her feel good? Has a friend ever said something nice to you? How did that make you feel?
Thursday	Philippians 2:3,4	Tell about a time when you let a friend go ahead of you or have the first choice. How did you feel at the time? What do you think God thought about your actions?
Friday	1 Samuel 16:7	When you are choosing a new friend, what should you think about? How can you tell who might be a good friend and who might not?
Saturday	Colossians 3:13	What should you do if a friend does something unkind to you?
Sunday	Galatians 1:10	Is it more important that we please God or that we do things so our friends will like us? Give an example.

Talking with God

Then you will call my name. You will come to me and pray to me. And I will listen to you (Jeremiah 29:12).

Pray this prayer or write your own prayer thanking God for His Word that teaches you how to be a good friend. Then spend some time praying together as you ask God to help you be a good friend to those around you.

Stuff We Need to Talk to God About

Think of one thing you need prayer for. Write it down in the space below. Talk about it together, and then remember to pray for each other this week.

Dear God,
Thank You for loving us and for giving us Your Son, the Lord Jesus Christ. Jesus is a great example for us to follow because He was a good friend to others. Help us to become more like Him. Thank You, God, for the Bible and that it teaches us how to treat others. Help us to be kind and caring. Help us to love our friends. Help us to forgive our friends when they hurt us. Thank You for the perfect gift of friendship. You are a great God! In Jesus' name we pray. Amen.

Daughter   **Mom**

Pray with all kinds of prayers, and ask for everything you need (Ephesians 6:18).

44

A Daughter's Reflection

God began doing a good work in you. And he will continue it until it is finished when Jesus Christ comes again (Philippians 1:6).

Read these questions aloud. Talk with your mom about your answer to each question. Draw or write about your answers to some of the questions in the space below.

1. What have you learned about friendship?

2. What can you do to become a better friend?

3. What does the Bible say about how a friend should act?

4. What is it like to have Jesus as your friend?

Backyard Garden Tea Party

I pray that your life will be strong in love and be built on love (Ephesians 3:17).

Make It Special

In addition to the tea party supplies and suggestions listed on pages 6 and 7, you can add a special touch to your Backyard Garden Tea Party with some of the supplies and ideas listed on this page.

❀ Set up a blanket or table and chairs in your backyard or at a nearby park.

❀ Display garden tools, seed packets, or backyard games on and around the tea party area.

❀ Make sun tea and serve it at the tea party.

❀ Work together to decorate an orange juice carton with construction paper and crayons. Pick a bouquet of flowers. Display the flowers in your vase at the tea party.

❀ Use markers on art paper to make flowery placemats.

❀ Wear clothing that has a garden or flower print design.

❀ Use art supplies to design colorful invitations, then invite your best friends to the tea party.

Tea Time Scripture

Talk about this Scripture verse while sipping your tea:

Every perfect gift is from God (James 1:17a).

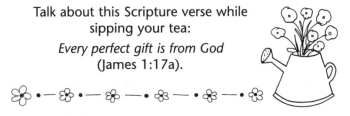

Try This

Try one or more of these activities to make your tea party extra special and more meaningful.

Friendship Activities

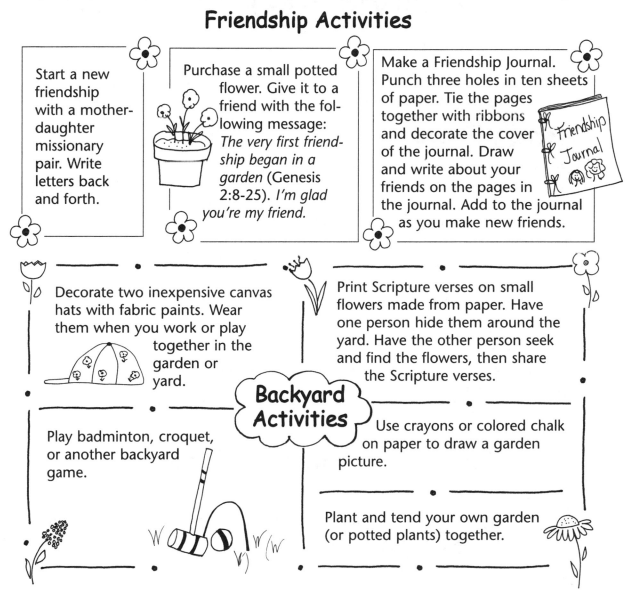

Start a new friendship with a mother-daughter missionary pair. Write letters back and forth.

Purchase a small potted flower. Give it to a friend with the following message: *The very first friendship began in a garden* (Genesis 2:8-25). *I'm glad you're my friend.*

Make a Friendship Journal. Punch three holes in ten sheets of paper. Tie the pages together with ribbons and decorate the cover of the journal. Draw and write about your friends on the pages in the journal. Add to the journal as you make new friends.

Decorate two inexpensive canvas hats with fabric paints. Wear them when you work or play together in the garden or yard.

Print Scripture verses on small flowers made from paper. Have one person hide them around the yard. Have the other person seek and find the flowers, then share the Scripture verses.

Backyard Activities

Play badminton, croquet, or another backyard game.

Use crayons or colored chalk on paper to draw a garden picture.

Plant and tend your own garden (or potted plants) together.

Menu Suggestions

Choose one or more of the following menu items. Work together to prepare the snack and then serve it at the tea party along with the tea, juice, or other favorite beverage.

Friendly Faces

Here's what you need: 10 mini rice cakes or round snack crackers, peanut butter, jam, cream cheese, butter knives, plates, small edibles such as raisins, chocolate chips, coconut, peanuts, small candies, and cereal pieces.

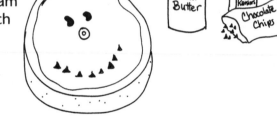

Here's what you do:
1. Spread jam, peanut butter, or cream cheese on each rice cake.

2. Add raisins, chocolate chips, nuts, etc. to make a friendly face on each rice cake.

3. Make a different face on each rice cake to represent you and your friends.

Fresh Fruit Flowers

Cut a variety of fruits into small pieces. Arrange the fruit pieces on skewers to look like an assortment of garden flowers.

Mom and Me

Chapter Three

Family Matters

> *It takes wisdom to have a good family. It takes understanding to make it strong. It takes knowledge to fill a home with rare and beautiful treasures* (Proverbs 24:3).

No matter the size of a family or if anyone shares the same hair color or eye color, there's no comfort in the world quite like knowing that you belong.

— ♥ Lori Wick

I Love My Family

Today I praise God for:

Praise and Thanksgiving

Praise God because he is great!...Lord, I will thank you with all my heart (Deuteronomy 32:3b and Psalm 138:1a).

Praise God for creating your family. Thank Him for each person in your home. Ask God to show you how to love your family better so you can make God happy.

Story Time

Samantha's Birthday

"Happy Birthday, Samantha! Happy Birthday to You," her family finished singing as Samantha blew out the candles on her cake. "You're the best daughter in the whole world," her mother whispered to Samantha, and then gave her a big hug.

It was Samantha's eighth birthday, and her family had planned a special party for her. They decorated the kitchen with balloons and streamers, bought some special snacks, and each person made her a birthday card. After playing games and eating cake and ice cream, Samantha sat down to open some gifts. Each person in her family gave her a gift and she loved them all.

After the birthday celebration the family gathered in the living room for devotions. Samantha looked at each person in her family and was thankful for them all. She told them so as she prayed that night.

"Dear God, thank You that it's my birthday and for the party I had today. I loved all the gifts. Most of all, thank You for the people in my family and the fun time we had together. My family is the greatest gift of all. You are a great God for creating all the special people in my family. Amen."

How about you? Are you thankful for the people in your family? Do you show or tell your family how much you love them?

The Bible Says,

Every perfect gift is from God (James 1:17).

Your family is one of those perfect gifts from God. Think about that as you work through this lesson together.

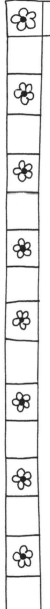

Let's Get Started

Directions: Use this recipe to make some modeling dough or purchase store-bought clay. Make each member of your family with the modeling dough. Then talk about the ways each person is special to you.

Modeling Dough Recipe

2 cups flour
1 cup salt
2 tablespoons oil
food coloring (about 4 drops)
water to moisten (about 1/2 cup)
assorted dry beans and seeds for decoration

Combine the first four ingredients. Add the water a little at a time. Mix to moisten until dough is of workable consistency. Store in an airtight container. Use dry beans, seeds, or other small objects to add detail to your people.

Sharing Our Thoughts

Most important, love each other. Use all wisdom to teach and strengthen each other (Colossians 3:14, 16b).

Read the questions below. Share your answers with each other and/or write down your answers in the spaces below.

1. What are some things you like to do with your family?

2. How can you show the people in your family that you love them?

3. Do you know someone who lives alone? What do you think it would be like if you didn't have a family?

4. Who was in the first family God created? (Hint: read Genesis 4)

ActivityTime

Family Prayer Basket

Materials needed:
- medium size basket
- 4-inch slips of paper
- artificial flowers
- 3x5 note card
- black marker
- bread twist tie
- yarn
- crayons
- ribbons

Directions:

1. Decorate the basket by winding the ribbons, yarn, or artificial flowers around the handle or edges of the basket.

2. Print your family name on the note card; then make a decorative border around the edge of the card with crayons or marker.

3. Poke a twist tie through the note card and attach it to the basket.

4. Decorate the border of each slip of paper and place them inside the basket along with the marker.

5. Tell your family about the prayer basket. Invite family members to write down specific prayer requests on the slips of paper and place them in the basket.

6. Each evening check the basket for prayer requests; then pray together about each person's request.

7. If there are no prayer requests in the basket, pray for each family member anyway.

The Murrays

❀Getting Into God's Word❀

Open my eyes to see the wonderful things in your teachings...How I love your teachings! I think about them all day long (Psalm 119:18, 97).

Read about how your family is a gift from God! Everyday this week read each Bible verse and answer the question(s). Share your answers with each other.

Day of the Week	Verse	Something to think about. . .
Monday	Proverbs 24:3,4	*What are some of the beautiful treasures in your home or family?*
Tuesday	Titus 2:3-5	*What are some things your mother has taught you?*
Wednesday	Ephesians 1:16	*What can you do for your family whenever you think about them?*
Thursday	1 Thessalonians 5:11	*What are some things you can do to encourage people in your family?*
Friday	Romans 12:10	*In what ways can you show honor to your mother and father?*
Saturday	Deuteronomy 6:6-9	*When does your family talk about God and His Word?*
Sunday	Genesis 2:18-23	*Why did God create women (Eve)? What are some ways your mom helps your dad?*

Talking with God

Then you will call my name. You will come to me and pray to me. And I will listen to you (Jeremiah 29:12).

Pray this prayer or write your own prayer, thanking God for your family. Then spend some time praying together as you ask God to help you love your family more.

Stuff We Need to Talk to God About

Think of one thing you need prayer for. Write it down in the space below. Talk about it together, and then remember to pray for each other this week.

Dear Lord,
Thank You for the people in my family. I love them very much. I praise You because I get to do fun things with my family. I love it when we go places together, and I especially like it when _____. Thank You for each person in our family including _____, _____, and _____. It's great to have people who will always love me and who will never leave me. Help me, God, to be better at showing love to the people I live with. Help me to be thankful for each person. Amen.

Daughter

Mom

Pray with all kinds of prayers, and ask for everything you need (Ephesians 6:18).

Mother's Insight

Share your personal thoughts with your daughter regarding one or more of the following questions or statements. In the space below write down some of your thoughts and ideas.

1. Share with your daughter about a time when you thought she made a special impact on your family.

2. Tell about a special memory of your family when you were growing up.

3. What are some things you learned from your mother that you want to teach your daughter?

4. Explain to your daughter about how important she is to your family.

A Family that Makes God Happy

Today I praise God for:

Praise and Thanksgiving

Praise God because he is great!...Lord, I will thank you with all my heart (Deuteronomy 32:3b and Psalm 138:1a).

Talk to God about how much you love your family. Thank Him for making each person in your family special. Praise God for your father and your mother. Ask God to help you obey your parents.

Story Time

The Soccer Team

Danielle loved soccer! She was on the red team, and her games were at 10:00 every Saturday morning. Danielle loved being part of a team. She knew that when she played on the team she had to remember her position. Every girl on the team had a different job to do. Laura was the goalie, Jordan was a forward, and her two best friends, Sophia and Melissa, were defenders. They each played a different position, but they had a common goal in mind: to play well, make points by scoring goals, and have fun!

Being part of a family is kind of like being on a soccer team. Each person on the "family team" has a different job or position (mother, father, daughter, son), and yet God created the family making each person equally important and valuable. And just like a soccer team, the family has one goal to accomplish together too: to love and serve God.

The Bible Says,

As for me and my family, we will serve the Lord (Joshua 24:15).

Think about how each person in your family has a different position or job and how your family works together to love and serve God.

Let's Get Started

Directions: Draw a picture of something your family does that shows you love God and want to serve Him better.

Our Family Loves God

Sharing Our Thoughts

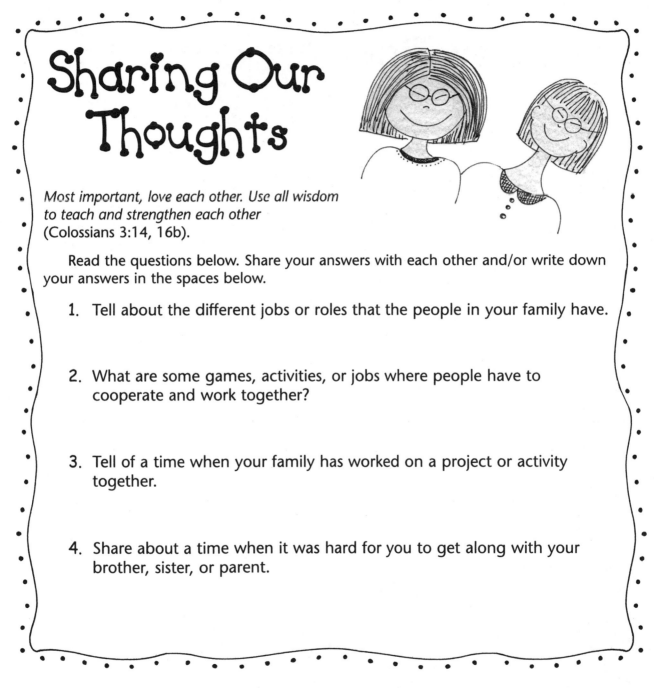

Most important, love each other. Use all wisdom to teach and strengthen each other (Colossians 3:14, 16b).

   Read the questions below. Share your answers with each other and/or write down your answers in the spaces below.

1. Tell about the different jobs or roles that the people in your family have.

2. What are some games, activities, or jobs where people have to cooperate and work together?

3. Tell of a time when your family has worked on a project or activity together.

4. Share about a time when it was hard for you to get along with your brother, sister, or parent.

Activity Time

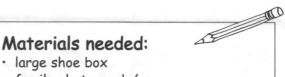

Familyscape

Materials needed:
- large shoe box
- family photograph (or drawing of your family)
- construction paper
- 3x5 note card
- (optional: non clasp wooden clothespins, craft paints, and yarn or fabric scraps)
- marker
- glue
- scissors

Directions:

1. Draw and cut pictures of furniture, windows, curtains, carpets, etc., from the construction paper.

2. Paste them inside the box so that it looks like a room in your home.

3. Display or glue your family photo inside the box. (Or make little people from the clothespins as shown; one to represent each person in your family. Glue them to the inside of the box.)

4. Fold the note card in half, so it will stand up.

5. Print *As for me and my family, we will serve the LORD* (Joshua 24:15) on one side of the folded card.

6. Display the verse inside the box.

7. Show the box scene to your family and tell them about what you learned in your lesson today.

Directions for making people:

Paint a shirt and pants on each clothespin. Use marker to draw facial features. Cut yarn or fabric and glue it to the top of the clothespin for hair. Let dry.

❀Getting Into God's Word❀

Open my eyes to see the wonderful things in your teachings....
How I love your teachings! I think about them all day long
(Psalm 119:18,97).

Read each day this week about how your family can please God. Read each Bible verse and answer the question(s). Share your answers with each other.

Day of the Week	Verse	Something to think about. . .
Monday	Luke 10:27	*The members of your family are your closest neighbors. How can you show love to specific people in your family?*
Tuesday	Romans 12:21	*If a brother or sister says or does something unkind to you, what can you do in return? Give a specific example.*
Wednesday	1 Peter 4:10,11	*How can you serve the people in your family?*
Thursday	Ephesians 6:1-3	*What are the children in a family supposed to do? How will you be blessed?*
Friday	Proverbs 31:27-30	*What are some ways you can show your mom you appreciate all she does for you?*
Saturday	Matthew 6:14	*If someone in your family hurts your feelings, what should you do? Explain why.*
Sunday	Ephesians 4:32	*What can you do to show kindness and compassion to the people in your family?*

Talking with God

Then you will call my name. You will come to me and pray to me. And I will listen to you (Jeremiah 29:12).

Pray this prayer or write your own prayer, thanking God for creating families. Then spend some time praying together as you ask God to help you become a family member that is loving and kind.

Stuff We Need to Talk to God About

Think of one thing you need prayer for. Write it down in the space below. Talk about it together, and then remember to pray for each other this week.

Dear God,
Thank You for creating families. It is great that You wanted a husband and a wife together, and then You blessed them with children. It is special to have other people to live with and to love. Thank You that I have a special part in this family. Thank You, Lord, that we can go to church together and pray to You. Help us to be a family that makes You happy. Help us to love each other no matter what. Amen.

Daughter   Mom

Pray with all kinds of prayers, and ask for everything you need (Ephesians 6:18).

A Daughter's Reflection

God began doing a good work in you. And he will continue it until it is finished when Jesus Christ comes again (Philippians 1:6).

Read these questions aloud. Talk with your mom about your answer to each question. Draw or write about your answers to some of the questions in the space below.

1. Why did God create families?

2. What do you like best about your family?

3. What have you learned about the people in your family and their specific role or job?

4. How can you do better at being part of your family?

Moonlit Night Tea Party

I pray that your life will be strong in love and be built on love (Ephesians 3:17).

Make It Special

In addition to the tea party supplies and suggestions listed on pages 6 and 7, you can add a special touch to your Moonlit Night Tea Party with some of the supplies and ideas listed on this page.

❀ Set up a blanket, or table and chairs outdoors on a warm night.

❀ Hang a string of white lights or Christmas lights near the tea party.

❀ Light a lantern or candle and set it in the center of the tea party table.

❀ Make and display *moonbeams*. Cut a moon shape from the front of a lunch bag. Pour rocks or sand in the bottom of the bag to keep it from blowing away. Set a 2-inch votive candle securely in the bottom of the bag. Light the candle. Make and display several *moonbeams* around the tea party area.

❀ Wear your best pajamas and slippers to the tea party.

Try This

Tea Time Scripture
Talk about this Scripture while sipping your tea:

He counts the stars and names each one. Our Lord is great and very powerful (Psalm 147:4,5a).

Try one or more of these activities to make your tea party extra special and more meaningful.

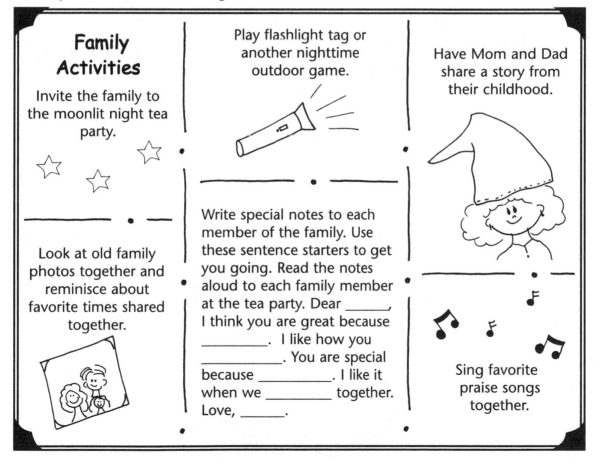

Family Activities

Invite the family to the moonlit night tea party.

Look at old family photos together and reminisce about favorite times shared together.

Play flashlight tag or another nighttime outdoor game.

Write special notes to each member of the family. Use these sentence starters to get you going. Read the notes aloud to each family member at the tea party. Dear _____, I think you are great because _____. I like how you _____. You are special because _____. I like it when we _____ together. Love, _____.

Have Mom and Dad share a story from their childhood.

Sing favorite praise songs together.

Nighttime Activities

Make simple nightcaps. Cut and sew two triangular shaped pieces of flannel together to fit your heads. Wear your nightcaps at the tea party. See sample on page 67.

Go on a Praise Walk: Shine a flashlight on something God has made and praise Him for creating it, for example: "Praise God for the flowers," "Praise God for the trees," etc.

Menu Suggestions

Choose one or more of the following menu items. Work together to prepare the snack and then serve it at the tea party along with the tea, juice, or other favorite beverage.

Favorite Family Recipe

Prepare one or more of your favorite family recipes and then serve them at the tea party as you talk about your family heritage and traditions.

Make S'Mores

Set a piece of chocolate bar between two graham cracker halves. Sandwich a roasted marshmallow between the two crackers and enjoy.

Try popping some microwave popcorn and serve it with hot cocoa.

Popcorn Time

68

Loving God's Word

Help me understand, so I can obey your teachings. I will obey them with all my heart. Help me obey your commands because that makes me happy (Psalm 119:34,35).

Is anything more wonderful than sitting in church with my daughter and having her touch my arm when the pastor quotes a verse that she has put to memory? The sparkle in her eye is worth every moment we spent working on it, even on days when she needed extra "encouragement."

— ♥ Lori Wick

Loving God's Word with All My Heart

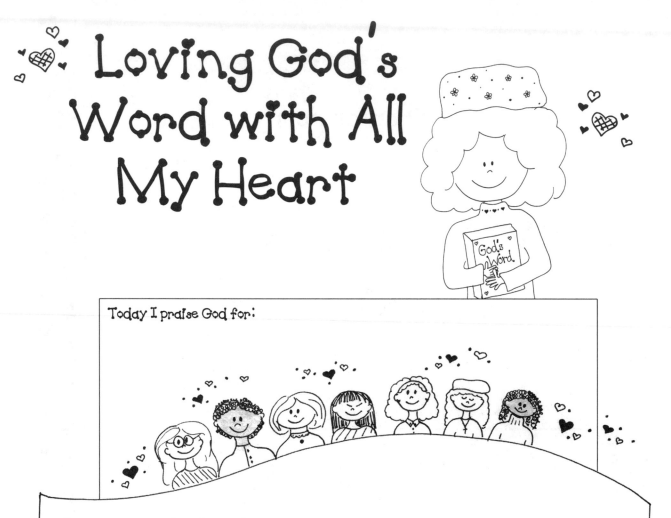

Today I praise God for:

Praise and Thanksgiving

Praise God because he is great!...Lord, I will thank you with all my heart (Deuteronomy 32:3b and Psalm 138:1a).

Praise God for creating the world and all that is in it. Thank Him for giving you His Word. Ask Him to help you love His Word so you can become more like Jesus.

Story Time

Freeze Pops and God's Word

Rose thought there was nothing better than eating a cold freeze pop on a hot summer day. "There are lots of reasons to love eating a freeze pop," she said. "They're fun to eat. They taste great. They cool you off, and sometimes they make your lips and tongue turn colors." She looked at her orange tongue in the mirror and smiled.

"Rose, it's time to practice your memory verse for Sunday school," her mother called from the living room.

Rose smiled at herself in the mirror, admiring her bright orange lips. She went to the living room and then snuggled on the couch with her mom. "The Bible won't make my tongue turn orange," Rose shared, "but I guess there are lots of reasons to love reading it."

Here are some great reasons for you to love God's Word:

❋ It helps you learn how much God loves you.

❋ It can make you happy when you're sad.

❋ It helps you get to know God better.

❋ It tells you how to obey God.

Can you think of other reasons to love God's Word?

The writer of Psalms wrote, *How I love your teachings! I think about them all day long* (Psalm 119:97).

Think about how you can learn to love God's Word more as you have fun on these activity pages.

☆ Let's Get Started ☆

Directions: Draw or write about a fun treat that you like to eat; then tell why you like it. List some reasons why you like reading God's Word.

A treat I like to eat is...

Here's why I like reading God's Word...

Sharing Our Thoughts

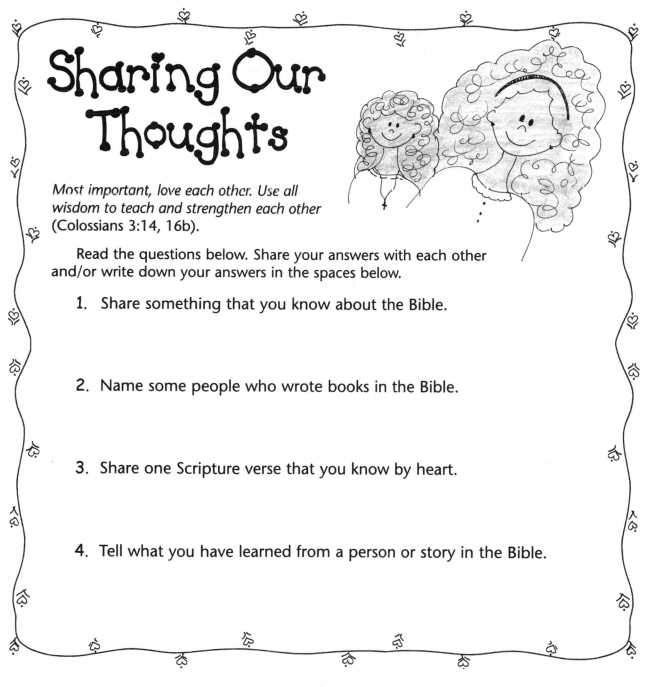

Most important, love each other. Use all wisdom to teach and strengthen each other (Colossians 3:14, 16b).

Read the questions below. Share your answers with each other and/or write down your answers in the spaces below.

1. Share something that you know about the Bible.

2. Name some people who wrote books in the Bible.

3. Share one Scripture verse that you know by heart.

4. Tell what you have learned from a person or story in the Bible.

Activity Time

All About Me Box

Directions:

1. Think of a favorite story or character from the Bible.

2. Create a puppet of that person(s) using the materials listed above. Make the puppet(s) as simple or elaborate as you like.

3. After gluing the materials to the bag, let the puppet(s) dry.

4. Use the puppets to present a puppet show to your family or friends, highlighting a specific Bible story or Bible verse.

Materials needed:
- brown paper lunch bags
- collage materials such as:
  - yarn
  - fabric scraps
  - construction paper
  - ribbon
  - buttons
  - ric-rac
- scissors
- glue
- markers or crayons

Alternative: Make stick puppets using tagboard and tongue depressors as shown, or make sock puppets using old socks, buttons, fabric scraps, yarn, and fabric paints.

King David

Mary

Getting Into God's Word

Open my eyes to see the wonderful things in your teachings...
How I love your teachings! I think about them all day long
(Psalm 119:18,97).

Read about God's great Book every day this week!
Read each Scripture passage and answer the question(s).
Share your answers with each other.

Day of the Week	Verse	Something to think about. . .
Monday	2 Timothy 3:16	*What are some ways God's Word is useful to you?*
Tuesday	Joshua 1:8	*If you think about God's Word often and are careful to follow it, what will happen?*
Wednesday	Isaiah 40:8	*What is one thing that will last forever?*
Thursday	Psalm 1:2	*What times in your day can you think and meditate about God's Word?*
Friday	Luke 11:28	*How do you feel when you obey God's Word?*
Saturday	Psalm 119:9-11	*How does memorizing Bible verses help you?*
Sunday	Psalm 119:105	*How is the Bible like a lamp or a light?*

Talking with God

Then you will call my name. You will come to me and pray to me. And I will listen to you (Jeremiah 29:12).

Pray this prayer or write your own prayer, thanking God for His Word. Then spend some time praying together as you ask God to help you love His Word more.

Stuff We Need to Talk to God About

Think of one thing you need prayer for. Write it down in the space below. Talk about it together, and then remember to pray for each other this week.

Dear God,
We praise You because You are awesome. Thank You for the Bible. Thank You that we each have a Bible and that we can take it wherever we go and read it. We love that Your Word teaches us more about You. Thanks for showing us how to love others by reading the Bible. Thank You for my teachers and parents who taught me how to read. Amen.

Daughter　　　　　　　　　　　**Mom**

Pray with all kinds of prayers, and ask for everything you need (Ephesians 6:18).

Mother's Insight

Teach older women to be holy in the way they live...In that way they can teach younger women (Titus 2:3,4a).

Share your personal thoughts with your daughter regarding one or more of the following questions or statements. In the space below write down some of your thoughts and ideas.

1. Share with your daughter about how you've seen her apply God's Word in her life.

2. Share about how God's Word has made a big impact on your life.

3. Tell how a specific Scripture verse helped you in a difficult time.

4. Share your thoughts on why it's important to make time to pray and read God's Word daily.

God's Word Is Great!

Today I praise God for:

Praise and Thanksgiving

Praise God because he is great!...Lord, I will thank you with all my heart (Deuteronomy 32:3b and Psalm 138:1a).

Thank God for giving you the great gift of the Bible. Praise Him because Scripture comes from the mouth of God. Thank God for teaching you how to live your life. Ask Him to help you obey His instructions.

Story Time

Read It Again!

"Read it again! That was a great book. I loved it. Can we read it again, please?" Carissa said after her teacher finished reading one of her favorite storybooks.

Have you ever said that after your mom or dad finished reading a story to you? Have you ever said those things after you heard a story from the Bible?

That's how God wants us to respond every time we read or hear His Word. He wants us to be excited about His Word and He wants us to love it. God's Book is greater than any book you'll ever check out from the library. It is a gift from Him. He wrote it for us, and we need to love it more than any book we have on earth.

The Bible Says,

Open my eyes to see the wonderful things in your teachings (Psalm 119:18).

Ask God to open your eyes to all the great things in His Book as you work through this lesson together.

Let's Get Started

Directions: Write your favorite book titles on the books in the space below.

Fill in the blanks of this poem with the following words; then read it aloud together.

- eyes
- hands
- body
- ears
- mouth
- mind

Loving God's Word with My Whole Self.

With my _____ I read His Word.

I use my _____ to hear.

With my _____ I tell my friends,

"God's Word is very near."

With my _____ I think of Him.

I clasp my _____ to pray.

I use my whole entire_____

to show God's love each day.

Sharing Our Thoughts

Most important, love each other. Use all wisdom to teach and strengthen each other (Colossians 3:14, 16b).

Read the questions below. Share your answers with each other and/or write down your answers in the spaces below.

1. Where is your favorite place to read your Bible?

2. Who do you like to read your Bible with?

3. Why do you like reading God's Word?

4. Tell about your favorite Bible story.

Activity Time

A New Psalm of Praise

Directions:

1. Cut the bottom off of the bag; then cut the remaining portion of the bag into two large pieces.

2. Tear a large rectangle from each piece of brown paper.

3. Use the black marker to write your own psalm on the paper, thanking God for His Word.

4. Crumble each piece of brown paper and squeeze it tight, then uncrumble it so that it looks like an old piece of parchment.

5. Praise God together as you read your new psalms aloud to the family this evening.

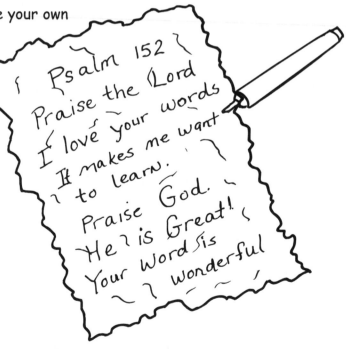

Psalm 152
Praise the Lord
I love your words
It makes me want
to learn.
Praise God.
He is Great!
Your Word is
wonderful

Getting Into God's Word

Open my eyes to see the wonderful things in your teachings...How I love your teachings! I think about them all day long (Psalm 119:18,97).

Read about loving God's Word every day this week! Read each Scripture passage and answer the question(s). Share your answers with each other.

Day of the Week	Verse	Something to think about. . .
Monday	James 1:22-25	*Why is it important to do what God's Word says and not just read it?*
Tuesday	Matthew 7:24	*What are some things you can do to build your life on the rock (Word of God)?*
Wednesday	Psalm 119:46-48	*How can you show you love God's commands?*
Thursday	Colossians 3:16	*How can you teach others about God's Word?*
Friday	Romans 15:4	*What are two things you have learned from God's Word?*
Saturday	Deuteronomy 30:11-14	*Why should you be thankful that you have your own copy of God's Word?*
Sunday	Matthew 4:4	*What are some things we need to stay alive physically? What do we need to stay alive spiritually?*

Talking with God

Then you will call my name. You will come to me and pray to me. And I will listen to you (Jeremiah 29:12).

Pray this prayer or write your own prayer, thanking God for giving you His Word. Then spend some time praying together as you ask God to help you make time to read His Word each day.

Stuff We Need to Talk to God About

Dear God,
Thank You that all Scripture comes from Your mouth. Lord, teach us about Your love in the Bible. Thank You for giving us instructions through Your Word with love, comfort, and encouragement. Help us, Lord, to make time every day to read Your letters to us. Your Book is greater than any other book we have. We love it. Amen.

Think of one thing you need prayer for. Write it down in the space below. Talk about it together, and then remember to pray for each other this week.

Daughter   **Mom**

Pray with all kinds of prayers, and ask for everything you need (Ephesians 6:18).

A Daughter's Reflection

God began doing a good work in you. And he will continue it until it is finished when Jesus Christ comes again (Philippians 1:6).

Read these questions aloud. Talk with your mom about your answer to each question. Draw or write about your answers to some of the questions in the space below.

1. Why should the Bible be your favorite book?

2. What would you say about the Bible to someone who has never read it before?

3. How can you show God that you are thankful for His Word?

School Days Tea Party

I pray that your life will be strong in love and be built on love (Ephesians 3:17).

Make It Special

In addition to the tea party supplies and suggestions listed on pages 6 and 7, you can add a special touch to your School Days Tea Party with some of the supplies and ideas listed below.

❀ Fill a school box with school supplies. Then tape a Scripture verse reference to each item in the box that pertains to learning and teaching about God's Word. Take turns removing the items from the box and looking up the verses. Read them aloud and talk about them. Here are a few to get you started: Romans 15:14; Proverbs 1:7,8; Proverbs 2:6; Luke 4:31,32.

❀ Display all the Bibles and Bible reference books from your home around the tea party area.

❀ Create a School Days centerpiece by arranging pencils, chalk, books, an apple, a lunch box, etc. in the center of the table.

❀ Cover the table with a large paper tablecloth or piece of butcher paper. Use markers to decorate the tablecloth with school days words and symbols, such as "2+2=4," "ABC," "123," "School is in session," "Recess!," etc.

❀ Make decorative napkin rings from colored construction paper. Print a Scripture verse on each napkin ring. Read your Scripture verse aloud as you open your napkin ring.

Try This

Try one or more of these activities to make your tea party extra special and more meaningful.

School Days Activities

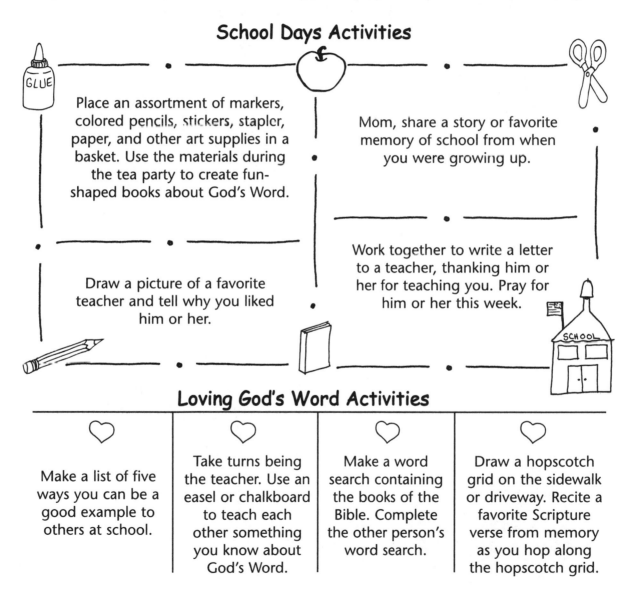

Place an assortment of markers, colored pencils, stickers, stapler, paper, and other art supplies in a basket. Use the materials during the tea party to create fun-shaped books about God's Word.

Mom, share a story or favorite memory of school from when you were growing up.

Draw a picture of a favorite teacher and tell why you liked him or her.

Work together to write a letter to a teacher, thanking him or her for teaching you. Pray for him or her this week.

Loving God's Word Activities

♡	♡	♡	♡
Make a list of five ways you can be a good example to others at school.	Take turns being the teacher. Use an easel or chalkboard to teach each other something you know about God's Word.	Make a word search containing the books of the Bible. Complete the other person's word search.	Draw a hopscotch grid on the sidewalk or driveway. Recite a favorite Scripture verse from memory as you hop along the hopscotch grid.

Menu Suggestions

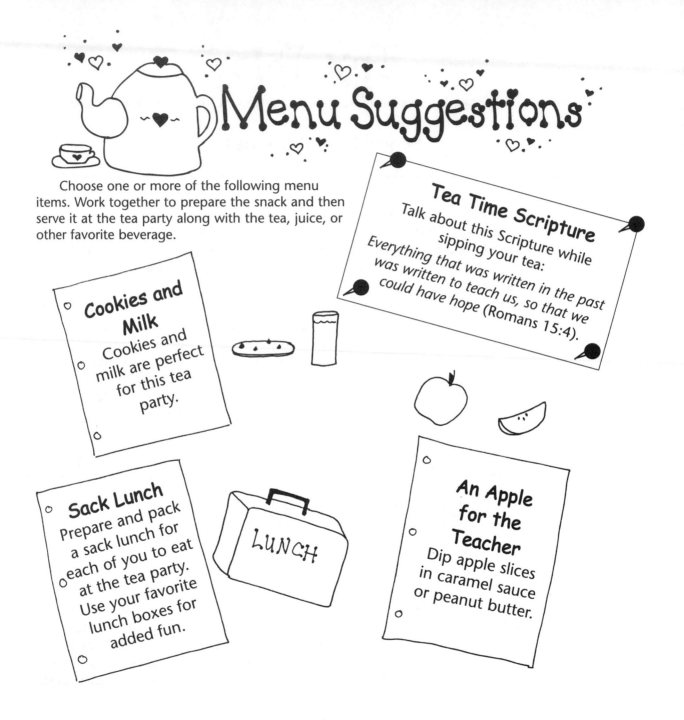

Choose one or more of the following menu items. Work together to prepare the snack and then serve it at the tea party along with the tea, juice, or other favorite beverage.

Tea Time Scripture

Talk about this Scripture while sipping your tea:

Everything that was written in the past was written to teach us, so that we could have hope (Romans 15:4).

Cookies and Milk

Cookies and milk are perfect for this tea party.

Sack Lunch

Prepare and pack a sack lunch for each of you to eat at the tea party. Use your favorite lunch boxes for added fun.

LUNCH

An Apple for the Teacher

Dip apple slices in caramel sauce or peanut butter.

Chapter Five

Getting to Know Our Awesome God

> Yes, I am sure that nothing can separate us from the love God has for us. Not death, not life, not angels, not ruling spirits, nothing now, nothing in the future, no powers, nothing above us, nothing below us, or anything else in the whole world will ever be able to separate us from the love of God that is in Christ Jesus our Lord (Romans 8:38,39).

"I didn't know that!" I've come to love those words from my daughter as we look into the Word and discover new truths about the awe-inspiring God we serve.

— ♥ Lori Wick

God Is Awesome!

Today I praise God for:

Praise and Thanksgiving

Praise God because he is great!...Lord, I will thank you with all my heart (Deuteronomy 32:3b and Psalm 138:1a).

What a great God we have! Praise Him for all the things He has done in the past and for everything He is doing in your life today. Thank God for giving you each other. Ask God to help you know Him better by reading His Word.

Story Time

My Dad Is Great!

"See ya, Dad! Have a good day at work," Kelly and Katrina called together. They had just finished swimming lessons. Their dad worked at the park taking care of the swimming pool and keeping the park clean. Kelly and Katrina loved their father. They thought he was the best!

"Isn't Dad the greatest?" Kelly asked. Her younger sister nodded in agreement. "Yeah, I especially like it when he lets me help him wash the car and I get to squirt him with the hose."

"I like it when he takes us fishing with him. Remember when I caught that eight-inch bass last year?" said Kelly.

Katrina responded, "Yeah, and Dad hardly ever yells at us. Plus, he comes to all of our swim meets."

Kelly and Katrina could think of lots of great things about their father.

"We do have a great dad," said Kelly, "but Katrina, we have an even greater Dad in heaven, don't we?"

"You got that right," said Katrina. "There are millions of things about God that make Him even greater than Dad."

The Bible Says,

Lord, there is no god like you. There are no works like yours. Lord, all the nations you have made will come and worship you. They will honor you. You are great and you do miracles. Only you are God (Psalm 86:8-10).

As you work through this lesson, think about all the things that make God great.

Let's Get Started

Directions: Draw and write about some things that make your dad great. (If you don't have a dad, write about a grandfather, brother, or favorite teacher.)

Sharing Our Thoughts

Most important, love each other.
Use all wisdom to teach and strengthen
each other (Colossians 3:14, 16b).

Read the questions below. Share your answers with each other and/or write down your answers in the spaces below.

1. Tell three reasons why you think God is great.

2. What are some great things God has done that you've read about in the Bible?

3. What are some neat things God has done in your life?

4. Is there someone in your life who needs to know how great God is? What could you say to them?

Activity Time

Bundle of Praise

Directions:

1. Cut a 12-inch square from the fabric.

2. Cut a piece of ribbon that is 14 inches long.

3. Use the permanent markers to print words that praise God on each stone, such as: *God is great. He is the Rock. God is faithful.*

4. Lay the fabric square on the table with the pretty side facing down.

5. Place the stones in the center of the fabric.

6. Gather the sides together and tie the bundle with the ribbon.

7. Make several Bundles of Praise.

8. Give these as gifts to friends or family members and share how great your God is.

❀Getting Into God's Word❀

*Open my eyes to see the wonderful things in your teachings...
How I love your teachings! I think about them all day long
(Psalm 119:18,97).*

Read about our great God every day this week! Read each Scripture passage and answer the question(s). Share your answers with each other.

Day of the Week	Verse	Something to think about. . .
Monday	Romans 8:28	*Tell about how God took something in your life that seemed "bad" and used it for good.*
Tuesday	Deuteronomy 31:6	*Why should we be strong and courageous?*
Wednesday	Colossians 3:12	*What can we do to show God that we love Him?*
Thursday	Psalm 136:1-9	*What are some of the great things God has done?*
Friday	Romans 8:38,39	*How do you feel knowing that nothing can separate us from God's love?*
Saturday	Psalm 145:1-3	*What are some ways you can praise God each day?*
Sunday	Philippians 4:19	*In what ways does God take care of you?*

Talking with God

Then you will call my name. You will come to me and pray to me. And I will listen to you (Jeremiah 29;12).

Pray this prayer or write your own prayer, praising God for who He is. Then spend some time praying together as you ask God to help you know Him better.

Stuff We Need to Talk to God About

Think of one thing you need prayer for. Write it down in the space below. Talk about it together, and then remember to pray for each other this week.

Dear God,
You are awesome. There is no one else like You. We praise You because You created everything and everything You made is good. Lord, we love You and want to live our lives so that You will be happy with us. We thank You for being a Father that loves us, forgives us, and blesses us in so many ways. Help us get to know You better as we spend time talking about You and reading Your Word. You are the only Great God and King. Amen.

Daughter   **Mom**

Pray with all kinds of prayers, and ask for everything you need (Ephesians 6:18).

Mother's Insight

Teach older women to be holy in the way they live...In that way they can teach younger women (Titus 2:3,4a).

Share your personal thoughts with your daughter regarding one or more of the following questions or statements. In the space below write down some of your thoughts and ideas.

1. Share with your daughter about a time when she taught you something about God.

2. What have you learned about God over the past several years that you didn't know when you were younger?

3. Tell about your salvation experience.

4. How have you seen God's power at work in a specific situation in your family's life?

5. How is God working in you? Explain how He has changed you over time.

God Loves Me!

Today I praise God for:

Praise and Thanksgiving

Praise God because he is great!...Lord, I will thank you with all my heart (Deuteronomy 32:3b and Psalm 138:1a).

Praise God for loving you so much. Thank Him for caring about every part of your life. Thank Him for loving you as His own child. Ask God to help you love others as He loves you.

Story Time

Cassandra's New Guinea Pig

Cassandra and her father were on their way home from the pet store. Cassandra had finally saved up enough money to buy herself a pet. She chose a big, round, furry guinea pig. His fur stood straight up, and Cassandra thought he was the cutest animal in the whole pet shop.

"Dad, I love my new guinea pig so much. I'm going to name him Fuzzball," Cassandra said, as they drove home with their new pet in the back seat. "And Dad, I just want you to know that I will take very good care of him. I'll make sure he has enough food and water. I'll give him lots of attention, and I'll never leave him alone. I just love him, Daddy! Thank you for letting me buy him." Cassandra then prayed quietly, thanking God for her new pet.

"Cassandra, you sure love Fuzzball a lot. You just made some pretty big promises," Dad replied.

"You promised to always care for him, always love him, and never to leave him alone. That reminds me of God's love for us. In the Bible, God tells us that He will always love us and that He will never leave us. He promises to meet all of our needs, to protect us, and watch over us. Your love for Fuzzball is great, and he's just an animal! Imagine how much greater God's love is for us."

The Bible Says,

The Father has loved us so much! He loved us so much that we are called children of God. And we really are his children (1 John 3:1).

Think about ways God shows His love for you as you work through these lessons.

Let's Get Started

Directions: Draw a picture of a pet that you have or would like to have. Draw or write about some ways you could love and care for that pet.

Sharing Our Thoughts

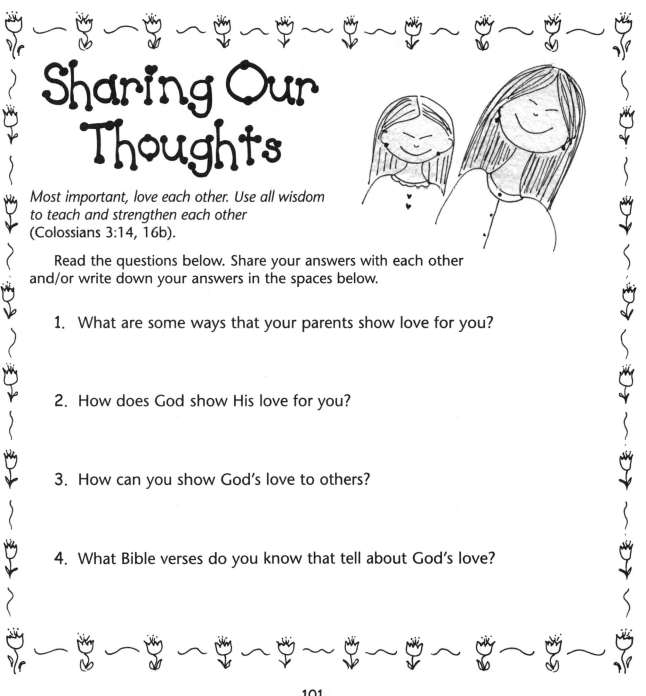

Most important, love each other. Use all wisdom to teach and strengthen each other (Colossians 3:14, 16b).

Read the questions below. Share your answers with each other and/or write down your answers in the spaces below.

1. What are some ways that your parents show love for you?

2. How does God show His love for you?

3. How can you show God's love to others?

4. What Bible verses do you know that tell about God's love?

Activity Time

Pocketful of God's Love

Directions:

1. Cut around the edge of each note card with the pinking shears and add a decorative border.

2. Print a Bible verse about God's love on each note card.

3. Use the art supplies to decorate the cards.

4. Have Mom use the needle and thread to sew each end of the shoelace to the inside of the pocket, to make a purse.

5. Use the fabric paints to print *God Loves Me!* on the pocket.

6. Let the fabric paint dry; then place the verse cards in your purse.

7. Carry it around as a reminder to show God's love to others.

Materials needed:
- 6 3x5-inch note cards
- needle and thread
- rubber stamp and stamp pad
- pinking shears
- back pocket from a pair of old blue jeans
- 36-inch shoelace
- stickers
- glitter
- markers
- fabric paints

His loving kindness will last forever.
Psalm 136

God Loves Me!

❀Getting Into God's Word❀

Open my eyes to see the wonderful things in your teachings.... How I love your teachings! I think about them all day long (Psalm 119:18, 97).

Read every day this week about how much God loves you! Read each Scripture passage and answer the question(s). Share your answers with each other.

Day of the Week	Verse	Something to think about. . .
Monday	John 3:16	*What is the greatest thing God did that shows His love for you?*
Tuesday	1 John 4:11	*How can you show your love for others?*
Wednesday	Isaiah 45:5,6	*What is special about our God?*
Thursday	Genesis 1:1	*What are some things that you see every day that show how great God is?*
Friday	1 John 1:9	*What does God do when you tell Him about your sins?*
Saturday	Hebrews 12:5-7	*Tell about a time when God or your parents showed their love for you by disciplining you.*
Sunday	Psalm 92:1-4	*What is one of your favorite praise songs to sing to God? How do you think God feels when we praise Him in song?*

Talking with God

Then you will call my name. You will come to me and pray to me. And I will listen to you (Jeremiah 29:12).

Pray this prayer or write your own prayer, thanking God for loving you. Then spend some time praying together as you ask God to help you learn how to show His love to others.

Stuff We Need to Talk to God About

Think of one thing you need prayer for. Write it down in the space below. Talk about it together, and then remember to pray for each other this week.

Dear God,
We praise You for being our Father in Heaven. Your love for us is so great. We love You too, God. Thank You so much for giving up Your Son, Jesus, so that we could live forever with You. You are powerful and wonderful. Help us to show Your love to others. We want others to know about how much You love them. Amen.

Daughter   **Mom**

Pray with all kinds of prayers, and ask for everything you need (Ephesians 6:18).

A Daughter's Reflection

God began doing a good work in you. And he will continue it until it is finished when Jesus Christ comes again (Philippians 1:6).

Read these questions aloud. Talk with your mom about your answer to each question. Draw or write about your answers to some of the questions in the space below.

1. What have you learned about God?

2. How can you get to know God better?

3. How does God show His love for you?

4. Tell about something God has helped you to do.

Rainbow Tea Party

I pray that your life will be strong in love and be built on love (Ephesians 3:17).

Make It Special

In addition to the tea party supplies and suggestions listed on pages 6 & 7, you can add a special touch to your Rainbow Tea Party with some of the supplies and ideas listed on this page.

❀ Wear bright and colorful clothing to the tea party.

❀ Display a large paper rainbow in the center of the table.

❀ Use a mix and match of colorful dishes, cups, saucers, and silverware.

❀ Sprinkle brightly colored dry cereal pieces or candies randomly about the table. Munch on these during the tea party.

❀ Cover the table with a brightly colored tablecloth, beach towel, or sheet.

❀ Print Scripture verses from this chapter that tell about our great God on colorful squares of paper. Display the squares randomly about the table, then read the verses aloud at the tea party.

Try This

Tea Time Scripture

Talk about this Scripture while sipping your tea:
I will announce the name of the Lord. Praise God because he is great! He is like a rock. What he does is perfect. He is always fair. He is a faithful God who does no wrong. He is right and fair (Deuteronomy 32:3,4).

Try one or more of these activities to make your tea party extra special and more meaningful.

Rainbow Activities

Use colored markers to write poems about color, rainbows, or God.

Paint rainbows on white paper with watercolor paints.

Have your daughter bring her most colorful beanbag pets to the tea party. Have each beanbag pet read aloud a passage of Scripture from this chapter.

Make Rainbow T-shirts. Use fabric paint or permanent markers to draw rainbows on plain colored T-shirts. Wear your shirts to the tea party.

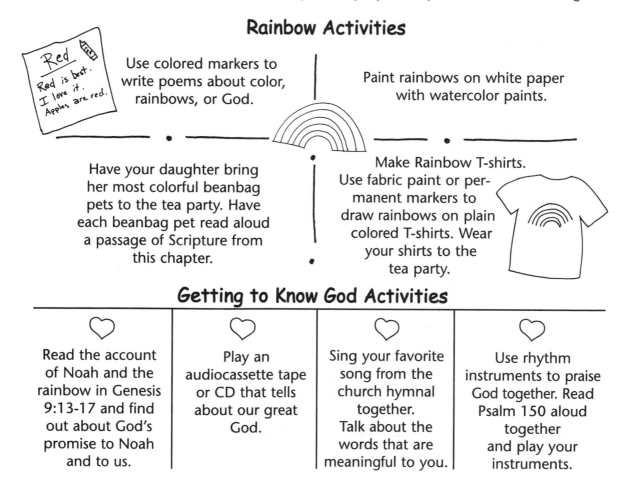

Getting to Know God Activities

♡	♡	♡	♡
Read the account of Noah and the rainbow in Genesis 9:13-17 and find out about God's promise to Noah and to us.	Play an audiocassette tape or CD that tells about our great God.	Sing your favorite song from the church hymnal together. Talk about the words that are meaningful to you.	Use rhythm instruments to praise God together. Read Psalm 150 aloud together and play your instruments.

Menu Suggestions

Choose one or more of the following menu items. Work together to prepare the snack and then serve it at the tea party along with the tea, juice, or other favorite beverage.

Edible Rainbow

Cut an assortment of fruits, vegetables, and cheese into bite-size pieces. Display the pieces in a rainbow formation on a large serving platter or plate. Then enjoy eating the rainbow together.

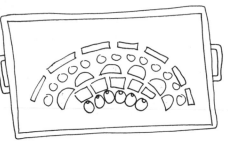

Rainbow Toast

Here's what you need: four plastic cups, 1 cup of milk, four slices of white bread, toaster, four clean paintbrushes, food coloring, butter.

Here's what you do:
1. Put 1/4 cup of milk in each cup.
2. Add one drop of food coloring to each cup of milk; then mix.
3. Use the brushes to paint a rainbow with the colored milk on each slice of bread.
4. Toast the painted bread. (The rainbow brightens up as it is heated.)
5. Top with butter and enjoy.

Helping Others

> When we have the opportunity to help anyone, we should do it. But we should give special attention to those who are in the family of believers (Galatians 6:10).

H stands for *h*ands that are willing to work.
E reminds us that *e*veryone's needs are important.
L stands for the *l*ove that prompts us to act.
P is for *p*leasing the Lord Jesus in all we say and do.

— ♥ Lori Wick

God Made Me to Be a Helper

Today I praise God for:

Praise and Thanksgiving

Praise God because he is great!...Lord, I will thank you with all my heart (Deuteronomy 32:3b and Psalm 138:1a).

Praise God for the help He gives you. Praise Him for making you a helper to others. Thank God for giving you so many opportunities to help people at home and in other places. Thank God for giving you Jesus as an example of someone who helped others.

Story Time

Eight Bags of Groceries

Jenna came home from school and found her mom in the driveway unloading groceries from the car. "Hi, Jenna, how was your day?" asked her mom.

"Pretty good I guess," she replied.

"Can you give me a hand with these groceries, Jenna?" her mom asked.

"Sure, Mom." Jenna counted...*6,7,8 bags.* "Boy, you bought a lot of food this time."

"Well I just wanted to make sure we had everything for the weekend camp-out and for next week's meals. You seem to be a little late today, Jenna. Is everything okay?" Her mother seemed concerned.

"Yeah. I just stayed after school a little while," Jenna said. "Alyssa missed the bus. She was crying a little bit, so I stayed with her until her mom picked her up."

"That was very kind of you. And Jenna, thank you for helping me with these groceries. You've been a big help. Let's go inside and share a soda and think of some ways you and I can help out the rest of the family tonight."

"OK, Mom." Jenna started to think about being a helper; then she said, "I bet I can help Joey with his homework. I can also offer to help Randi clear the table, even though it's her turn. Maybe you can help Dad by listening to him tell about his day at work."

"Those sound like great ideas to me," said Mom. "Come on, let's go. We have lots of helping to do around here."

The Bible Says,

When we have the opportunity to help anyone, we should do it (Galatians 6:10).

Think of ways you can help others as you work through this lesson.

Let's Get Started

Directions: Look at the two girls in the pictures below. What might each girl be saying about helping others? Write their words in the dialogue bubbles.

Sharing Our Thoughts

Most important, love each other. Use all wisdom to teach and strengthen each other (Colossians 3:14, 16b).

Read the questions below. Share your answers with each other and/or write down your answers in the spaces below.

1. What are three things you can do to help family members? Be specific.

2. Tell about a time when you were able to help someone at school or work.

3. How do you feel when you help other people?

4. Share a favorite Bible story that tells about people who helped each other.

Activity Time

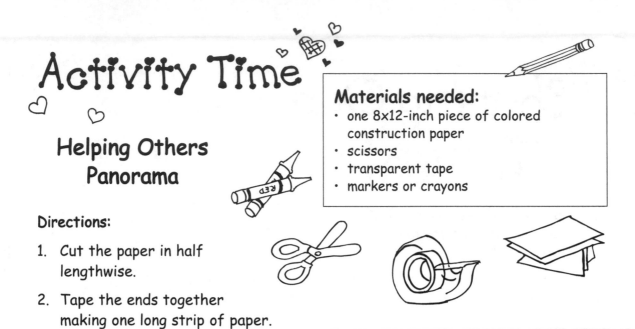

Helping Others Panorama

Materials needed:
- one 8x12-inch piece of colored construction paper
- scissors
- transparent tape
- markers or crayons

Directions:

1. Cut the paper in half lengthwise.

2. Tape the ends together making one long strip of paper.

3. Fold the paper accordion-style every three inches.

4. Print *I Can Help Others* in the first space.

5. Draw a picture of yourself helping a different person in each of the five remaining spaces.

6. Display the panorama in your bedroom as a reminder to help others.

Getting Into God's Word

Open my eyes to see the wonderful things in your teachings. How I love your teachings. I think about them all day long (Psalm 119:18,97).

Read about how you can help others every day this week! Read each Bible verse and answer the question(s). Share your answers with each other.

Day of the Week	Verse	Something to think about. . .
Monday	Luke 10:30-37	What did the Samaritan do to help the injured man?
Tuesday	Exodus 20:12	What are some ways you can help your parents that will show you honor them?
Wednesday	Ephesians 2:10	What are some good works God has prepared for you to do?
Thursday	Genesis 2:18-21	What are some things a wife can do to help her husband?
Friday	Colossians 3:17	Who should you be trying to please when you are helping others?
Saturday	Matthew 25:35,36	What are some ways you can help others according to these verses?
Sunday	Proverbs 31:10-30	What are some ways this mother helps her family? How does your mom help your family?

Talking with God

Then you will call my name. You will come to me and pray to me. And I will listen to you (Jeremiah 29:12).

Pray this prayer or write your own prayer, thanking God for making you a helper. Then spend some time praying together as you ask God to help you think of ways you can help others with a joyful heart.

> Dear God,
> Thanks for giving us a job to do. Help us, Lord, to find ways to help people. We want to help others because we know it makes You happy. Lord, help us to have a happy heart when we help other people and not to complain about it. Thank You for working in our hearts so that we can become more like You. In Jesus' name we pray. Amen.

Stuff We Need to Talk to God About

Think of one thing you need prayer for. Write it down in the space below. Talk about it together, and then remember to pray for each other this week.

Daughter   **Mom**

Pray with all kinds of prayers, and ask for everything you need (Ephesians 6:18).

Mother's Insight

Teach older women to be holy in the way they live...In that way they can teach younger women (Titus 2:3,4a).

Share your personal thoughts with your daughter regarding one or more of the following questions or statements. In the space below write down some of your thoughts and ideas.

1. Encourage your daughter by reminding her of a time when she was a good helper to someone.

2. Share about a time when you were able to help someone.

3. Tell of a time when you needed help and someone was there to help you.

Helping Others Pleases God

Today I praise God for:

Praise and Thanksgiving

Praise God because he is great!...Lord, I will thank you with all my heart (Deuteronomy 32:3b and Psalm 138:1a).

Thank God for the Bible that teaches you how to be a helper. Ask Him to give you a heart that likes to help other people. Ask God to show you ways that you can help each other throughout the week. Thank Him for the people in your life who help you.

Story Time

The Folding Party

Anna Marie flopped onto the couch to watch her favorite television show. Her mother came in and set down a big basket of clean laundry that needed folding. "Time for a folding party, Anna Marie. Would you mind helping me fold this laundry before you watch that show?"

"Oh, Mom, do I have to?" sighed Anna Marie. "I only want to watch for a half hour. Besides, I've been in school all day. Can't you do it?"

"Anna Marie, you are not talking kindly right now. Please turn off the TV!" Anna Marie obeyed her mother, but she wasn't very happy about it.

"Anna, God wants you to joyfully obey me and to help out when it's needed. You can't just think of yourself. And you didn't talk respectfully to me. Now please, let's fold these clothes together; then we'll be done quicker."

"OK, Mom," Anna said. Anna Marie prayed silently to God as she folded, "Lord, please help me to want to be a good helper to my mother."

After a few quiet moments Anna spoke up, "Did you know Jonathan brought in his pet grass snake today? We each got to hold it. It was neat. And Patti fell off the swings today at recess. They had to take her in for stitches. It was kind of an exciting day! Mrs. Cook was gone too, so we had a substitute teacher. That was fun."

"Thanks for sharing with me, Anna Marie. And thanks for helping with the folding. I know God is pleased with your joyful attitude."

"You know, Mom, that TV show isn't that important anyway. I'd rather help you any time," Anna Marie smiled.

The Bible Says,

Try to learn what pleases the Lord (Ephesians 5:10).

Think about being a helper that pleases the Lord as you work through this lesson.

:Let's Get Started:.

Directions: Draw and write about ways that Jesus pleased God by helping people.

Jesus pleased God by helping others.

Sharing Our Thoughts

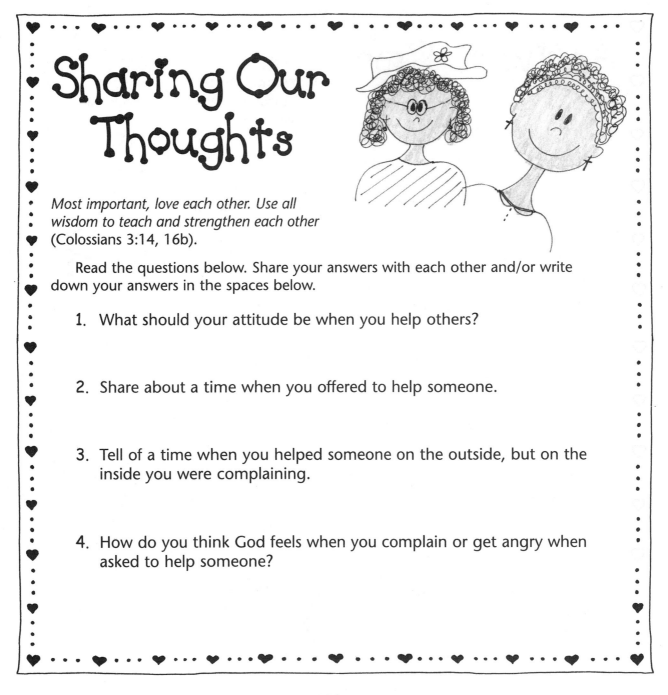

Most important, love each other. Use all wisdom to teach and strengthen each other (Colossians 3:14, 16b).

Read the questions below. Share your answers with each other and/or write down your answers in the spaces below.

1. What should your attitude be when you help others?

2. Share about a time when you offered to help someone.

3. Tell of a time when you helped someone on the outside, but on the inside you were complaining.

4. How do you think God feels when you complain or get angry when asked to help someone?

Activity Time

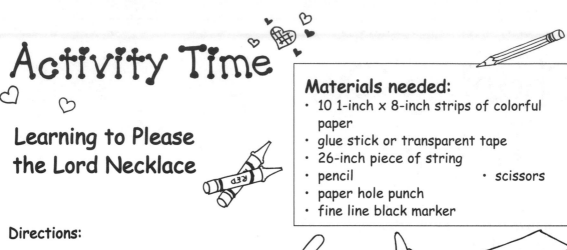

Materials needed:
- 10 1-inch x 8-inch strips of colorful paper
- glue stick or transparent tape
- 26-inch piece of string
- pencil
- paper hole punch
- fine line black marker
- scissors

Learning to Please the Lord Necklace

Directions:

1. Cut a heart shape from the note card.

2. Punch two holes in the top of the heart as shown.

3. Print *I'm learning to please the Lord* on the heart in fancy writing.

4. To make beads: Roll each strip of paper tightly around a pencil, then tape or glue the end.

5. Push the bead off of the pencil and let it dry, (if you used glue).

6. Use the black marker to add polka dots or designs to each bead.

7. String the beads and the heart onto the string as shown (right).

Getting Into God's Word

Open my eyes to see the wonderful things in your teachings....
How I love your teachings! I think about them all day long
(Psalm 119:18,97).

Read about how helping others makes God happy!
Read each Bible verse and answer the question(s).
Share your answers with each other.

Day of the Week	Verse	Something to think about. . .
Monday	**Deuteronomy 6:18**	*What are some good deeds you can do that will help others?*
Tuesday	**1 Corinthians 10:33**	*What is one important reason we are to help people, especially those who don't believe in God?*
Wednesday	Luke 17:11-19	*Jesus helped ten men. How did the one man respond to Jesus? How can you respond when someone helps you?*
Thursday	**Luke 10:38-42**	*How could Martha have asked for help in a nicer way?*
Friday	**1 John 3:17,18**	*Tell about a time when you or your family helped someone in need.*
Saturday	**1 Timothy 4:12**	*Even though you are young, what are some ways you can help others learn about God?*
Sunday	John 5:1-8	*How did Jesus help the man? How does Jesus help you?*

Talking with God

Then you will call my name. You will come to me and pray to me. And I will listen to you (Jeremiah 29:12).

Pray this prayer together or write your own prayer. Talk to God about how you want to be a helper that pleases Him.

Stuff We Need to Talk to God About

Think of one thing you need prayer for. Write it down in the space below. Talk about it together, and then remember to pray for each other this week.

Dear God,
We know that You have given us the job of helping others. Thank You for that opportunity. Help us, Lord, to want to please You and not ourselves. Help us to give up things we want to do so that we can give someone else a helping hand. Thank You that Jesus shows us how to help others. Thank You for the strength You give us each day to show your love. Amen.

Daughter   **Mom**

Pray with all kinds of prayers, and ask for everything you need (Ephesians 6:18).

A Daughter's Reflection

God began doing a good work in you. And he will continue it until it is finished when Jesus Christ comes again (Philippians 1:6).

Read these questions aloud. Talk with your mom about your answer to each question. Draw or write about your answers to some of the questions in the space below.

1. Why do you like to help people?

2. How can you do better at helping others at home?

3. What does God think when we help others with a joyful heart? With a complaining heart?

Teddy Bear Tea Party

I pray that your life will be strong in love and be built on love (Ephesians 3:17).

Make It Special

In addition to the tea party supplies and suggestions listed on pages 6 and 7, you can add a special touch to your Teddy Bear Tea Party with some of the supplies and ideas listed on this page.

- ❀ Gather all your teddy bears together. Set them around the room and at the tea party table. Give each bear a small paper cup to hold his "tea."

- ❀ Wear an article of clothing or accessory that has a teddy bear theme.

- ❀ Set several smaller teddy bears in the center of the table with the teapot and serving tray.

- ❀ Make teddy bear place cards: Cut teddy bears from wrapping paper, wallpaper scraps, old birthday cards, or use rubber stamps. Paste each bear to a folded 3x5-inch note card. Print each person or bear's name on a place card and then set them around the table.

Tea Time Scripture

Talk about this Scripture while sipping your tea:

Let us think about each other and help each other to show love and do good deeds (Hebrews 10:24).

Try This

Try one or more of these activities to make your tea party extra special and more meaningful.

Teddy Bear Activities

♥ Make simple clothing for your teddy bears to wear to the party. Cut a rectangular-shaped piece of fabric to the size of each bear. Cut out two armholes. Cut a belt from the same fabric. Wrap the clothing around the bear, put his arms through the holes, and tie the belt around the waist.

♥ Invite two friends (a mother/daughter pair) to the teddy bear tea party. Have them bring their favorite teddy bears.

♥ Tell which teddy bear is your favorite and why.

♥ Read a favorite bear book together, such as *Corduroy* or *Winnie the Pooh*.

Helping Others Activities

Make a list of ways you can help people in your family and neighborhood in the upcoming week.

Make simple note cards from construction paper and art supplies. Draw a teddy bear on each card, then write a note of encouragement to someone who needs cheering up.

Ask each other, "What's one thing I can do for you each day that would help you?" Try to do that one thing faithfully throughout the week.

Make a blank book. Title it: *Jesus Helps People. I Can Help People Too.* Draw pictures and write about ways that Jesus helped people and ways you can help people too.

Menu Suggestions

Choose one or more of the following menu items. Work together to prepare the snack, and then serve it at the tea party along with the tea, juice, or other favorite beverage.

Honey Triangles

Here's what you need: four slices of white bread, honey, butter knife, plate.

Here's what you do:
1. Cut the crust off of four pieces of white bread.
2. Spread honey on each slice.
3. Cut each slice into four small triangles.

Teddy Bear Dips

Here's what you need: teddy bear-shaped cookies, semi-sweet chocolate chips, glass bowl.

Here's what you do:
1. Melt the chocolate chips in the microwave (about 60 seconds).
2. Dip each bear cookie into the melted chocolate until half of the cookie is covered with melted chocolate.

Let dry on a sheet of waxed paper for about ten minutes; then arrange the cookies on a plate.